STAYING ALIVE
LAURA SIMS

STAYING ALIVE
LAURA SIMS

UGLY DUCKLING PRESSE, 2016

First Edition, First Printing, 2016
Edition of 1400

ISBN 978-1-937027-62-9
Distributed by SPD / Small Press Distribution
www.spdbooks.org

Ugly Duckling Presse
The Old American Can Factory
232 Third Street #E-303
Brooklyn, NY 11215

Design by Don't Look Now!
Typeset in Univers

Covers printed letterpress at UDP
using polymer plates from Boxcar Press.
Printed and bound at McNaughton & Gunn
on acid-free, partially recycled paper.

Ugly Duckling Presse is a member of the
Community of Literary Magazines and
Presses and a 501(c)(3) registered nonprofit.
Tax-deductible donations are welcome.

This book is made possible in part by a
grant from the National Endowment for
the Arts, and by continued support from
the New York State Council on the Arts.

www.uglyducklingpresse.org

ART WORKS.   NYSCA

CONTENTS

for Caleb

ONE

"I want to go ahead of Father Time
with a scythe of my own."

— H.G. Wells

By the bountiful lake of your torso, the ships arrive.

In a seemingly endless

Glittery line

Linens air out

Nonetheless. Will it

Ends and another thing ends

But you   you

Fawn on the ground in the shape of your

Basest self. It's an infinite

Blur? The future

Empty

Of children

The present sheared

Asunder from its parent cliffs and all the past was just

The sound of metal

Warming

At the edge of space

At dawn. Every blasted city

Stilled—

The light! It came from *underneath*—inside the earth—

And shining upward, through

The rocks, the ground, and everything

Down the ill-made road, minds swaying

Our batteries

What is that

Flicker in the sky

That swift liquefaction

That masked and expectant

Black muzzle

That overhead the dawn

That limbs and tentacles, followed by

Night

And a devil of a row

A prolonged ululation: pantry vessels

Ring and shift as the social body

Is

Gutted, slashed

And gutted

The earth became a sea that rocked our house and power

Fled the grid and pummeled

Into me

The red glow from the East the burning docks

A boat with no one on it brought

A startling, sharp joy: behold

The searchlights'

Lustrous

Fugitive

Humanity

The young ones came in the gloaming

Dolled up

In three puffs of green smoke. They produced

A deep sound

Amidst supping and lovemaking. Invisible

Hands lit the bushes

Astonishment

Turned

Into something

Wet leather

Where men

Had stood for a moment, a moment ago

This little world: the smell

Of dead meat, and the giant

Machines

[Suddenly, all of it seemed like a dream. I flung myself

Underwater and heard

A man

Who sounded

Like a siren]

The rose-colored foot

Of the Martian

Fell
like a
garment a
grotesque
mingling
my wife's
face
white
but
a ruin
the sodden
man between

*

Not simply torn between longing and safety

But torn

I became

One of them, leaning over the railing

And no one would help

The humans left

Not even the humans

In puddles and mud

In mittens and coats

Lies my tribe

Without, the strange wonder

Of dreams and lusts

Moved

Among brutes

The place rocked

With that beating thud and it

Rained down darkness as we made our

Miserable

Skedaddle

When I

Sat by the brightness / slew by the brightness / I slew

The last curate whose wailing

Possessed me. Useless and cumbersome

Empire

or

Bouquets of fire

We gathered provisions:

A clock, a slipper

And a silver spoon

We happened on no dead

Instead we happened on a man whose palms

Filled with berries. We packed up our needs (amid vapor

And smoke) to make for the virtual fortress. In a sliver

Of light, something crystal

Or crystalline

Graced the court of manhood then was gone

One hand beat

At a guttering softening bellying eddying

Bank of white dust

Swift

Spreading coils

Our men and

The source of our decadence—all of deep space—extracted

At last to a

Wilderness

The world

Burns best

When its soft mass, intact

Is lashed, pinned or woven to deepening whiteness

The darker

The night grooves the face of the world and

Clean snow stifles the cavity

The city teems. Above

It isn't heaven: it's

The ruin

Where

You shine

We gave our meat to the meat plant

& the garden, town, village

Lifted from the mind

*

From above we saw:

A ruined shape

We turned to [colorless]

The sea was like the sky   a long,

Long chain that tethered everything

TWO

"Things were a little better and a lot worse.
In the ruins of the city another city was
built, and then another, and another,
none more golden than any other."

— Eliot Weinberger, *Karmic Traces*

COLOSSAL   FIGURES   OBSCURED BY MIST

"The world can't possibly fail"

We had the wild feeling of burning

A final machine. Far back

In the Year of the Lions.

We had the wild feeling of harnessing

The fury of the boars. And then (against the quiet hum

The gods reared up a new people from stone

When the culture passed over

We bathed   in its light   in its fear   in its

Mountain stream. We left mountains

Of carts full of junk behind. We bade them

Farewell. They bade us

Weep and know shame

They bade us be hard.

Without power, I wielded my body

My nerve

Rattled through me

Behind it

Was land—behind that was the Zone

The trees were scarred too

They were washing the streets with white powder

—Look—

Smoke pouring into the universe

The air	full	of sound
The air	full	of sound
The air	full	of sound
The air		of sound
The air	"AN	of sound
The air	EVACUATION	of sound
The air	IS	of sound
The air	A	of sound
The air	TERRIBLE	of sound
The air	THING"	of sound
The air		of sound
The air	full	of sound
The air	full	of sound
The air	full	of sound
The air	full	of sound
The air	full	of sound
The air	full	of sound

Radioactive   ambulances   apples

Hanging

In the garden

The growing desert

Of houses:

Words

Between a person and her soul

Oh strange person

Oh person in a vacuum

We with our cannons and spaceships were children

Somewhere below

The great Mother of Cities

Here it's the same

And the atom is everywhere

*

What stood in our yard were like demons
outside of time. One had a rock in its mouth,
another a tree branch.

"[By] the smoky flame of the lamp they licked spoons

"[By] the ring of blue teeth [they] tipped bowls [and they] drank the rich
   syrup

"[He] wrapped him and wrapped him

"The flame puttered out

"Come down

"Oh my god

"And see

The mind burns

Time. The mind

Burns time and its bygones

Look

I am semblance

Of life I am

Shaped like a rock like dirt vegetation and urban debris

*

The great machines

Make greater machines

And so on

At last, at last

To hunger and terror

Salami and buckwheat

We'll stand between death and its shining ideals

We'll fatten from hunger and light the whole earth

With our comrades' debris

We'll be grim set on living

We'll bury the headquarters, schools, and the baths

And the water main

THREE

"He ceased to be lost not by returning
but by turning into something else."

— Rebecca Solnit,
A Field Guide to Getting Lost

Down a wide staircase of marble is

Nothing but waste. Any sojourn out there (to the stars)

Will report nothing and

Nothing

And nothing. I grab her hair in both hands

It feels good. That we are at home with the

Red & white stars

Her genes & mine

I squint and the city revives. I am suddenly

Bustling. Basket in hand. Among others

We were lost

From the city. We were somehow

Suspended in air. We were

Part of her throng

Wearing makeup and she

Wore makeup as never before.

I said her name loudly. And then she appeared

In the book's illustrations

Spreading honey all over her chest

She walked up to me and spread honey all over her chest

Star wars & ax wars & the letting of blood

The last beast dies.

And under the "starry arch of heaven"

And in the "stony Middleworld of earth," and even

In the "dark waters of the Underworld,"

We celebrate

Over the phonograph. How the tune it plays

Echoes wetly. Like we're

Underwater again in the days

When the sky was a crocodile, like we're

The ones thinning the membrane: the beast

Comes back, comes slithering

The last ferry is

Drowning its riders

In dust and in

Space

In the Winter Garden
In the Winter Garden
I wander the Winter Garden with you

Palm trees have risen

Again

And the last

Chandeliers

Suspend

The eye must follow

The polestar, bright

Out of twilight. It seems to rise, to move

From side to side, to sink. The sky

It keeps receding. Now the world is soaked

Remote

You have a pebble in your mouth. One day you may find

Yourself alone on such a raft

The land. The grass. The wagon. The wind. The land. The road.

The trees.
The sound.
The water.

The rider.

Wild

Animals. The trace. The wheels.　　　The fire. Space. The bowl.

There was only: a pale pink glow
Above pink was yellow
Above yellow was blue
Above blue was no

Color at all

*

The campfire lost its shady groves and its rushing sound

Trees hung over it
Cooling

The great sky emptied its bowl of light onto wild

Grasses and buffalo. It pushed us west and then

Slowly the land became black

The wind made a sound, small and lost in such space

            Here grew   the tall trees

     Here hung   the large stars

In the groves they lay down, the invisible animals

What shines

And flutters in the water there

Since man came groping

Tidbits of bone or

A fat red sirloin

Forked on a stick

A small dark head

Most graceful of watercraft

Tossed

Like a gourd in a lake

Let the hot clean stones

Be a wilderness

Filter, let them clatter

Against cave walls

Drink blood

From the glacier, scooped out by hand

Let it quiet the mind

Let the quiet mind quiet the body

The quelled body

Disquiets the mind

You were always a murmurous forest

But now you are

This

                    Incandescence

This slim

Conflagration

As long as

Your body

As brief as your body, it

Sputters

And gasps until

Oil runs over the bones

The young lie so fearlessly

White and gelatinous

Slit from vent to throat

If I had needed meat

If I had wanted glossy fur

Bright buckets echo

The plunder bogs down while the spring sap comes rising

The clean bitter tang

Burns like a torch

In the Silent Places

I'm fuel

For felling I'm

Deadfall

In heaven

I'm plastic

Somehow

Where the melting sun

Only one time

In thousands

Makes of me

What swells

Then subsides

Those are my molecules, stopping the tides

This

My mind

Returned

*

The hollow feeling on the far side of the moon

We chased from the school

A wolf and a she-wolf

Through deep forest aisles through

Opaque cones of smoke

*

We drew close to something then

We who don't live

On this earth

AFTERWORD

The clocks stopped at 1:17. A long shear of light and then a series of low concussions. He got up and went to the window. What is it? she said. He didn't answer. He went into the bathroom and threw the lightswitch but the power was already gone. A dull rose glow in the windowglass. He dropped to one knee and raised the lever to stop the tub and then turned on both taps as far as they would go. She was standing in the doorway in her nightwear, clutching the jamb, cradling her belly in one hand. What is it? she said. What is happening?

I don't know.

Why are you taking a bath?

I'm not.

—Cormac McCarthy, *The Road*

When I first read *The Road* seven years ago, it filled my dreams and my waking life and lingered for weeks after I'd finished. To be more precise: I *let* it fill my mind, I let it haunt me, because I had the freedom to immerse myself in what I perceived to be a frightening vision of humankind's future, before I'd had a child. Just after my son was born, I relegated *The Road*—with its roving gangs of kid-eating cannibals, among other terrors—to the fog-shrouded back of my brain where such things can go missing. All that lingered were a few key scenes and my sense of the book's dark, appealing density. Picking it up again now, several years later, I find *The Road* transformed—from a book filled only with darkness, fear, death, and sorrow, to one focused on the survival, however fraught and tenuous, of humankind. Reading it now, I see that what matters in the above scene from *The Road* is not the world-ending event only glancingly referred to, but the primary human anxieties pulsing to life: the anxiety of parenthood (*cradling her belly*), the anxiety of ignorance (*What is it? What is happening?*), and the anxiety caused by sudden, unexpected helplessness (*the power was already gone*). And what matters more is what the humans do in response to these driving anxieties—like the father-to-be, who drops to one knee to start to keep them alive.

My son, now five, has started to ask probing existential questions on a regular basis. "Do old persons not have bones?" he asks. "Were we alive in the old days?" "What happens to people who die?" And, "What's at the end of space?"

Guy Davenport, in his afterword to Ronald Johnson's God- and Satan-less *Radi os*, writes this about the state of interplanetary travel and the investigation into our existence as universal beings:

> As I write this a spaceship is circling Mars. . . . It will report back . . . that there is nothing there but desolation. A similar voyage to all the other planets will report nothing, nothing, nothing. That we are alone in a universe of red stars and white stars, a catastrophe of light and electric thunder of time, vibrant forever, forever bright, fifty-eight sextillion, seven hundred quintillion, seven hundred and sixty quadrillion miles wide (by Einstein's reckoning), is the plain fact our age will have to learn to live with, as Milton in his lifetime had to learn that the earth is a planet of the sun, a smallish star.

Nine years since Davenport wrote this, however, the Mars Curiosity Rover has discovered evidence of dried water sources and other components of life, such as carbon, oxygen and hydrogen. What may have been life-sustaining bodies of water at one time may have lasted millions of years.

The Chernobyl Exclusion Zone, once home to 120,000 people, has become, in the years since the 1986 disaster, a sort of thriving nature preserve. A 2011 *Wired* article notes that wolves, lynx, and elk now roam the area under whose soil lies the bulldozed and buried radiated topsoil of the Zone. "It seemed the disaster that had banished industry, agriculture, pesticides, cars, and hunting from Chernobyl had inadvertently created a sprawling wildlife park," the author notes. Although scientists have found that some species have been afflicted with tumors, albinism, deformed body parts, and infertility, images captured online by cameras hidden in the Zone look like those you might see from inside Yellowstone.

In George R. Stewart's science fiction classic, *Earth Abides*, a disease wipes out most of the world's human population. Animal populations rebound and overrun San Francisco, a city now almost emptied of human inhabitants. "As for man," the narrator ruminates, "there is little reason to think that he can in the long run escape the fate of other creatures, and if there is a biological law of flux and reflux, his situation is now a highly perilous one. . . Biologically, man has for too long a time been rolling an uninterrupted run of sevens."

If human beings suddenly vanished from the earth, Alan Weisman posits in *The World Without Us*, there is little chance of our fellow inhabitants, the animals, missing us. Dogs and horses "would miss the steady meals," but dolphins, elephants, pigs and monkeys, the animals we consider most intelligent, "probably wouldn't miss us much at all." "Mainly," he writes, "we'd be mourned by creatures who literally can't live without us because they've evolved to live on us: *Pedicululs humanus capitis* and her brother *Pediculus humanus humanus*—respectively, head and body lice."

But I don't really care what the animals would think, or how they would thrive in our absence; instead, I cling to *The Road*. One day, when the father and son are on the verge of starvation, they discover a fallout shelter in someone's backyard, stocked with canned goods and a cooking stove, cots and folded clean blankets. They sink into the place with deep relief (as do we). They eat. Bathe. Sleep. We revel in the luxuriant details that follow: the boy's clean hair, his newly washed jeans, his full belly, the lamplight.

In the Chernobyl Exclusion Zone, before it became the Chernobyl Exclusion Zone, "we churned our butter ourselves, our cream, made cottage cheese, regular cheese. We boiled milk dough . . . We drank juice from birch and maple trees. We steamed beans on the stove. We made sugared cranberries. And during the war we gathered stinging-nettle and goose-foot. We got fat from hunger, but we didn't die."

Time magazine's online pictures gallery of Chernobyl twenty-five years after the disaster shows us shredded books layering the floor of a school, an abandoned ferris wheel of an amusement park that was set to open a week after the disaster, an empty swimming pool, doors left forever standing open, chipped murals, rusted beds from what was once a kindergarten, and a blasted-out window looking out on stark, abandoned Soviet buildings. I prefer these images of inanimate objects and empty places to the pictures of the animals; they allow me to project my own mourning for the loss of human activity onto the things themselves. *You see*, they attest, *the world regrets your absence.*

. . .

In the wake of 9/11, "reconstruction of the [World Financial Center's] Winter Garden required 2,000 panes of glass, 60,000 square feet of marble flooring and stairs, and sixteen 40-foot *Washingtonia robusta* palm trees at a cost of $50 million." When I visited the refurbished Winter Garden with my best friend and my then one year-old son in

2011, we gazed in awe at the deserted atrium, at its polished marble floors and majestic palm trees, its windows to the sky. But when we wandered down a hallway off the atrium, we found rooms full of debris and disrepair, reminders of the past carnage and persistent decay. We stood there for a long time, staring at the bald truth of the place—at the broken mirror propped against a wall, the tattered armchairs, and the dust-covered chandelier crookedly at rest on a large, round table—until we'd seen enough. We turned our backs on the room, returned to the sunlit Winter Garden, marveled at the grandeur, the expense, and the vast and echoing beauty of the place, all of which said: the end of something never happened here.

I have tried to find evidence of this visit. I distinctly remember being there, snapping photos of the atrium and back rooms. I can recall the feel of the place, the drifting emptiness of those rooms, the instant dejection I felt on standing there, the disjunction between them and the spacious atrium. But my friend doesn't remember going there at all, and I can't find the pictures I took anywhere in my carefully archived photo collection. They could be lost in the vast scores of photos I keep. They could be mislabeled or I could even have deleted them because I thought they were insignificant. Ugly. Disturbing. Better to remember the flawlessly restored palms and the view of blue sky. But there are no pictures of those either.

. . .

In a rare dream I once had about my dead mother I met her in a sort of afterlife, after the fall of a civilization or at the dawn of a new one—or maybe at the intersection of both. She stood on a wide, windswept balcony welcoming me with her generous smile. I peered over the edge of the balcony and saw fallen columns scattered on the hillside below. Saplings and wildflowers had grown up amidst them in the days, weeks or years since they'd fallen. I took my mother's hand in the dream to show her I would stay, I would be with her in this place, but when I looked down at my hand, I was somewhere down below, on a dusty road, holding the handle of a basket. Preparing to shop in the rustic marketplace nearby. When did I choose this life over that one? I craned my neck to see the balcony up there, in the clouds.

. . .

"Were we alive in the old days?" My son asks. "What were people made of in the old days?" "In their caves were they wearing their skins and bones?" "Were they eating the animals with hands and teeth?" "What was it like inside their skin? Inside their blood?"

No, I tell him. Skin and muscle and bones, like today. Yes, I say. Yes. I don't know. I don't know. It was like being inside our skin, our blood, only different.

"Since man came groping out of the cold of fireless eons," as Bradford Angier notes in *How to Stay Alive in the Woods*, we have needed fire, water, food and shelter. I find the book's solid advice soothing—it explains how to hunt frogs with a spear (and first, how to make the spear), how to collect birch syrup, what plants are safe to eat (clover but not buttercups), how to build a "death pit" for animals, where to find and how to filter potable water, how to use bark as a water container, what kind of wood burns best, how to make a house out of snow, how to make a signal fire (if there's anyone left to signal), how to survive an avalanche or quicksand or snakebites or wolves.

When the world (as we know it) ends, and if we survive, we can return to the forests, meadows, lakes and mountain streams. We can eat what we've killed and gathered with our own hands. We can huddle together for warmth around the cave fire. We can raise our children close to the earth, weave clothes from grasses and animal skins, paint words and images on cave walls, make love on a dirt floor, kill wild game with bows and arrows, speak with our eyes and hands only, bathe in newly fresh streams, and boil drinking water for purity. This is pure hokum and fantasy, of course: the life I've described, culled from survival idylls like *Robinson Crusoe* and *Swiss Family Robinson*, would mostly be wretched and hard.

> A long time ago, when all the grandfathers and grandmothers of today were little boys and little girls or very small babies, or perhaps not even born, Pa and Ma and Mary and Laura and Baby Carrie left their little house in the Big Woods of Wisconsin. They drove away and left it lonely and empty in the clearing among the big trees, and they never saw that little house again.

The prose of the opening sequence of *Little House on the Prairie* has a biblical feel to it; it sounds like *Genesis*, though it is more about exodus. But genesis follows exodus here: "They were going to Indian Country." They were heading towards a new life, one that seems alien to us now: the pioneer life, something akin to my post-apocalypse fantasy life. They would live with a kettle over the fire, wind through the cracks between the logs of their cabins, handmade cotton clothes and blankets, slabs of fresh meat cut from animals killed by Pa, fresh fruit from the orchard and vegetables from the garden, picked by the girls and canned by Ma, satisfying outdoor labor and deep, rejuvenating sleep. But the novel touches on the harsh realities of pioneer life, too, since Wilder knew them firsthand: sickness and frequent death, confrontations with the Native Americans whose lands they were poaching, long, rough winters and unrelenting labor. Even so, *Little House* remains an intoxicating vision of a fresh world, a clean slate, one that is hard to resist. Hard not to long for, even if it never existed, and never could, in the wake of whatever may come.

I've spent many weeks, months and years of my life worrying about the end. Which is just a roundabout way of worrying about death, I suppose, though it feels grander. More global. Important. There are so many ways it could go—an asteroid could collide with the earth, or a rogue black hole could breeze through the Milky Way, destroying us all. An engineered virus could run rampant, or we could see the rise of a naturally occurring plague. We could run out of food, water and fossil fuels as the warming earth's population continues to expand. Aliens could invade. Killer robots could take over. Environmental toxins could kill us. The world could end in all-out nuclear war. "We removed our glasses after the first flash," William L. Laurence writes of witnessing the 1945 bombing of Nagasaki.

> Observers in the tail of our ship saw a giant ball of fire rise as though from the bowels of the earth, belching forth enormous white smoke rings. Next they saw a giant pillar of purple fire, 10,000 feet high, shooting skyward with enormous speed . . . Awe-struck, we watched it shoot upward like a meteor coming from the earth instead of from outer space, becoming ever more alive as it climbed skyward through the white clouds. It was no longer smoke, or dust, or even a cloud of fire. It was a living thing, a new species of being, born right before our incredulous eyes.

The earth's ultimate end will happen with or without continued human habitation. "In 5 billion years, the fuel in our Sun will begin to die and expand, becoming a red giant. At some point, our oceans will boil away. No one on Earth will be alive to see a red glow filling most of the sky," writes Clifford A. Pickover, author of *The Loom of God: Mathematical Tapestries at the Edge of Time*.

As he walked on the moon in February of 1971, Edgar D. Mitchell, NASA pilot, "realized that the molecules of my body, the molecules of the spacecraft, and those of my partners had been prototyped in some ancient generation of stars. And, okay, that was nice intellectual knowledge, but all of a sudden it hit me at the gut, and—wow—*those are my molecules.*"

September 2015

AUTHOR'S NOTE

Some of the words, lines, images and ideas in *Staying Alive* were informed by and/or appropriated from the following books, articles, films and TV shows: *Voices from Chernobyl: The Oral History of a Nuclear Disaster*, by Svetlana Alexievich (Trans. Keith Gessen); *How to Stay Alive in the Woods*, by Bradford Angier; *Conversations on the Edge of the Apocalypse*, Ed. by David Jay Brown; *Childhood's End*, by Arthur C. Clarke; "Afterword" to Ronald Johnson's *Radi os* by Guy Davenport; *Forest of Kings: The Untold Story of the Ancient Maya*, by David Freidel; "Is Chernobyl a Wild Kingdom or a Radioactive Den of Decay?" by Adam Higginbotham (*Wired*); *The End of the World*, ed. by Lewis Lapham; *Wittgenstein's Mistress*, by David Markson; *The Road*, by Cormac McCarthy; *After the Ice: A Global Human History 20,000-5,000 BC*, by Steven Mithen; *Tropic of Chaos: Climate Change and the New Geography of Violence*, by Christian Parenti; *A Paradise Built in Hell: The Extraordinary Communities that Arise in Disaster*, by Rebecca Solnit; *Earth Abides*, by George R. Stewart; *The World Without Us*, by Alan Weisman; *The War of the Worlds*, by H.G. Wells; *Little House on the Prairie*, by Laura Ingalls Wilder; "Winter Garden Atrium" (Wikipedia); *9* (Dir. Shane Ackerman); *Battlestar Galactica* (2004-2009); *Cave of Forgotten Dreams* (Dir. Werner Herzog).

ACKNOWLEDGMENTS

My deepest thanks to Matvei Yankelevich and to the members of the UDP collective who helped make this book.

A selection of poems from *Staying Alive* was published in a beautifully handmade chapbook, *POST-*, by Goodmorning Menagerie Press in 2012. Individual poems first appeared in the following journals: *Black Clock*, *Black Warrior Review*, *Broome Street Review*, *Chicago Quarterly Review*, *Denver Quarterly*, *Eleven Eleven*, *Fact-Simile*, *Gulf Coast*, *Omniverse*, and *Turbine*.